D0432215

MAR   2005

Why the West was Wild

Wayne Swanson

ANNICK PRESS

TORONTO + NEW YORK + VANCOUVER

Annick Press Ltd.

We acknowledge the support of the Canada Council for the Arts, the Ontario Arts Council, and the Government of Canada through the Book Publishing Industry Development Program (BPIDP) for our publishing activities.

Editing by Pam Robertson
Copy editing by Elizabeth McLean
Cover design and interior design by Irvin Cheung/iCheung Design

Cover illustration based on *In Without Knocking* by Charles Russell
Back Cover illustration based on *The Bucking Bronco* by Charles Russell

Every effort has been made to trace copyright holders and gain permission for use of the images within this book. If there are any inadvertent omissions we apologize to those concerned and ask that they please get in touch with the publisher.

The text was typeset in Sabon, Corporate, Interstate, and Harlem

Cataloging in Publication

Swanson, Wayne
    Why the West was wild / Wayne Swanson.

Includes index.
ISBN 1-55037-837-6 (bound).—ISBN 1-55037-836-8 (pbk.)

    1. West (U.S.)—Social life and customs—19th century—Juvenile literature. 2. Frontier and pioneer life—West (U.S.)—Juvenile literature. 3. West (U.S.)—History—19th century—Juvenile literature. I. Title.

F591.S92 2004   j978'.02   C2003-905820-4

Printed and bound in Belgium

Published in the U.S.A. by
Annick Press (U.S.) Ltd.

Distributed in Canada by
Firefly Books Ltd.
66 Leek Crescent
Richmond Hill, ON
L4B 1H1

Distributed in the U.S.A. by
Firefly Books (U.S.) Inc.
P.O. Box 1338
Ellicott Station
Buffalo, NY 14205

Visit our website at: www.annickpress.com

About the Author

Wayne Swanson has always enjoyed reading about the adventurous people and dramatic events that shaped the West. He was inspired to bring the stories to life for a new generation after visiting the Autry Museum of Western Heritage in Los Angeles, California. *Why the West was Wild* is his first book for young readers.

Contents

Building the West

"GOLD! GOLD!" It was 1848, and newspaper headlines were announcing the discovery of amazing riches in California, grabbing the attention of adventurers around the world. Masses of people started flooding to the West to seek their fortunes. They dreamed of wealth, not only from gold, but also from the farmlands, fish, and forests that were rumored to be there just for the taking. Within four decades, settlers had transformed the West from a vast, wild land to a booming part of the continent, and in the process, they created one of the most exciting periods ever in North American history.

BY THEN, AMERICANS were ready to push across the Mississippi to the untamed lands in the West. They had won the war against Mexico, taking ownership of the southwest, including California. And they had settled their boundary with Canada, adopting Washington and Oregon as territories. For the first time, the Pacific Ocean washed against American soil, and politicians wanted settlers in those new territories. They offered cheap—even free!—land to those willing to go west.

After all, eastern North America wasn't the paradise it had once been. A growing population had increased the competition for work. Not only were jobs scarce because of a depression that followed the war with Mexico, but the East was also running out of available farmland.

No wonder newspaper slogans, such as "Go West, young man," spurred so many people to act. They were willing to leave friends and family behind and risk dangers unknown to follow their dreams—to start new lives in a "land of opportunity."

But filling dreams was not easy. The West was an untamed land—a wild, wild place. Why? In part because there were few laws to protect people. Settlers fought other settlers and Native people over rights to the land. Thieves stole gold, cattle, and cash. Professional gamblers swindled money from free-spenders. And the law was that of the gun, where scores were often settled with a bullet rather than in court. Stories of the wild West fascinated people in the East, and many Westerners became legends in their own time.

This book looks at some of the characters who made the West wild: rugged miners, fierce warriors, hard-riding cowboys, surly outlaws, and brave lawmen. It tells stories of starvation, war, murder, gunfights, and hangings— events that have captured the attention of generations and still fascinate us today.

Between 1850 and 1890, the West grew from roughly 1 percent to more than 20 percent of the U.S. population.

Frederic Remington, *The Quarrel*

Migrants who often suffered from famine and religious persecution in their homelands jumped at the chance for a better life in America's West

After the American Civil War (1861–1865) between the pro-slavery southern states and anti-slavery northern states, many people moved west in search of free land and better opportunities than those in the war-ravaged east.

Pike's Peak or Bust, 1860

Oregon City

Fort Walla Walla

OREGON TERRITORY

UNORGANIZED TERRITORY

MINNESOTA TERRITORY

Mississippi River

SOUTH PASS

Salt Lake City

Sacramento

San Francisco

UTAH TERRITORY

IOWA

Fort Laramie

Nauvoo

ILLINOIS

Independence

CALIFORNIA

MISSOURI

Los Angeles

Santa Fe

Fort Dodge

ARKANSAS

San Diego

NEW MEXICO TERRITORY

TEXAS

THE WESTBOUND TRAILS

- Oregon Trail
- Sante Fe Trail
- Mormon Trail
- Gila River Trail
- California Trail

THE MAJOR MIGRATION TRAILS OF THE WEST

Unknown Land

As exciting as their dreams were, pioneers in the 1840s feared what might lurk beyond the next hill. They had been awed by tales of fierce tribes that roamed the plains, hunting gigantic herds of buffalo. They had heard that the Native peoples were often at war with one another and that their war parties traveled great distances to attack neighboring tribes. Pioneers believed these warriors could just as easily attack them.

POWERFUL NATURAL FORCES also threatened wilderness travel. Wherever the pioneers looked, they could see nothing but seas of grass, fuel for sweeping fires. On the open plains, they could be hammered by hailstorms and devastated by tornadoes. They had to trudge across vast stretches of land with little water for drinking or cooking, and few trees to provide relief from the searing sun.

As they continued west, the pioneers could see mountains: breathtaking to look at, but treacherous to cross by wagon. They could be caught in sudden blizzards in rugged passes, or forced to cross fast-flowing mountain streams. Without roads or bridges, they would have to shoot the rapids of the Columbia River with their wagons tied to crude rafts.

The whole time, they would be on their own, far from any communities. At the time the first wagon train started out, only a few hardy settlers had moved into four states along the west bank of the Mississippi River and pockets of land farther west.

The pioneers' limited knowledge of what lay ahead came from explorers and fur traders who had ventured into the wilderness. They had no accurate maps to help them find their way. And there were no towns where they could get directions or take on fresh supplies—only the odd trading post that bartered with Natives for furs. These isolated traders had little to offer weary pioneers on their trek.

Despite their fears about this unknown land, early pioneers saw it as a challenge on their way to heaven. They believed in Manifest Destiny, the idea that God wanted the U.S. to create a land of liberty from the Atlantic to the Pacific. Convinced they had a right to the bounty of the western lands, they were willing to face whatever they must to get it.

Charles Russell,
Trouble on the Horizon, 1893

Kit Carson

Kit Carson, a mountain man who had roamed the plains trapping furs, gained fame when he scouted for John C. Frémont's expeditions to Oregon and California. Together, they mapped the South Pass, the easiest route through the Rockies for the wagon trains.

Settlers threatened the survival of many nomadic tribes by killing buffalo and spreading deadly diseases, such as measles and smallpox.

Comanches, a Native people who lived mainly in Texas, were excellent riders and fierce warriors. Their war parties rode great distances to stage raids on pioneers' wagons.

Uinta Ute warrior and his bride, northwest Utah, 1873

A Navajo family, Canyon de Chelle, New Mexico Territory, 1873

Arthur Tait, *Life on the Prairie: The Trappers Defence, "Fire Fight Fire"*

Crossing the Continent

Dust filled the sky as 60 "prairie schooners"—covered wagons loaded with goods—and 5,000 cattle, horses, mules, and oxen churned up the prairie sod. The wagon train stretched along the horizon as far as the eye could see. Many pioneers walked beside their wagons to avoid choking on the rising dust. It would take them almost six months to cross the seemingly endless plains and mountains.

EVEN JUST REACHING Missouri, the starting point of the trek, was a long journey for many pioneers. Each spring, until 1869, they gathered there to form wagon trains. As long as they traveled in groups, they felt safe from attacks by Natives. Every night, they placed the wagons in circles for added protection.

But the Natives they feared often proved to be more of a help than a danger. Some tribes guided the pioneers and helped them cross raging rivers. The pioneers also depended upon the Native people to provide food and deerskin clothing in exchange for iron goods, such as pots.

Even so, many pioneers didn't survive the long trip. The trails were lined with gravesites—1 pioneer in 17 died, mainly from accidents or disease. Months of plodding also wore out the wagons and weakened the animals so they could no longer pull heavy loads.

Wagons and furniture were dumped because the owners simply couldn't cart them any farther.

In 1858, a faster, but more expensive, way to cross the continent arrived. For $200, Butterfield Stagecoach Lines took passengers from Missouri to California in just three weeks. In each coach, as many as 21 travelers (9 on three benches inside and up to 12 on top) jostled along, stopping at 139 stations along the way for meals and sleep. However, pioneers who journeyed by stagecoach were limited to one small bag each—hardly enough to begin a new life.

Mail also had to travel across the continent. Beginning in April 1860, Pony Express riders delivered important messages by horseback between San Francisco, California, and St. Joseph, Missouri, in only 10 days. Riders carried a lightweight mail pouch at full gallop for roughly

120 kilometers (75 miles) at a stretch, changing horses every hour or hour and a half. By passing the pouch from rider to rider, they kept the mail moving nonstop, usually covering a total of 400 kilometers (250 miles) a day. As great as this service was, the completion of the telegraph line put the Pony Express out of business 18 months after it started.

Not only did better and faster technology end the Pony Express, it also killed travel by wagon train. In 1869, work crews completed the first transcontinental railroad, making the prairie schooner obsolete.

In 1846, blizzards stranded 89 members of the Donner Party in the Sierra Nevada Mountains. Cold and snow killed many of them, but 45 people survived by eating the bodies of those who had died.

Traveling by stagecoach, 1889

A Mormon family rests in front of their wagons

In 1847, religious leader Brigham Young led 148 Mormons in 72 wagons to the Great Salt Lake Valley. He founded Salt Lake City as a place where his followers could live without fear of persecution.

"Pony Bob" Haslam was one of the gutsiest Pony Express riders. Hit by Natives' arrows and bullets, he once rode 190 kilometers (120 miles) with a broken jaw and a shattered arm.

Frank Tenney Johnson, *Trouble on the Pony Express,* ca. 1910–1920

Buffalo Hunters

Pounding hooves shook the ground as gigantic herds of buffalo raced across the plains. The stampede thundered over rolling hills—one solid, moving mass covered the landscape. Eager young men sent from the wagon trains to bring back meat for supper stared in amazement. They had never seen such large animals, let alone a herd that size. However, as more and more covered wagons and livestock followed, they soon destroyed the grasses that the giant buffalo needed to survive, driving the mighty herds away from the wagon trails.

NATIVE HUNTERS, WHO chased the massive animals across the plains, hunted with special "buffalo horses." With superior speed and stamina, these horses were able to carry their riders close to fleeing buffalo, yet swerve just in time to avoid the animals' sharp horns. Horses also helped Native people move their camps more easily, allowing them to follow the herds year round.

The Plains Natives thrived on buffalo, getting almost everything they needed from the animals. They turned hides into tipis, blankets, and clothes; sinews into bowstrings; horns into cups and arrow points; and bones into scrapers. Of course, they also depended on buffalo meat. What they didn't eat immediately they dried or mixed with fat (and sometimes dried berries) to make pemmican.

By the time wagon trains began arriving, Native people knew which of the settlers' goods they wanted to trade for. They had already begun to offer buffalo to traders on steamboats along the Missouri River. These traders exchanged guns, knives, whiskey, coffee, and sugar for hides, encouraging Native hunters to kill far more buffalo than they needed to survive.

Eventually, non-Native hunters also began to slaughter buffalo, especially for the hides that tanneries bought to make leather. They ventured out for weeks at a time with teams of skinners. A skilled hunter using a big gun could shoot 100 buffalo a day, but would leave most of the meat to rot.

Other hunters also began to butcher large numbers of buffalo. Railroad companies even offered excursions to tourists wanting to shoot from trains just for the thrill of it. They also hired professional hunters to get meat for their workers. One of their best hunters, William Cody, earned the name "Buffalo Bill" by single-handedly killing thousands of buffalo to feed the railroad crews.

Overhunting began to seriously thin the herds. By 1890, the number of buffalo had fallen drastically, from 60 million to a mere 1,000. Hunters had driven this giant of the plains nearly to extinction.

Buffalo Bill

Buffalo hide yard in 1878, showing 40,000 buffalo hides, Dodge City, Kansas

Major General William T. Sherman

Before Spanish explorers brought horses to North America, the Natives hunted buffalo on foot, often by chasing them over cliffs called buffalo jumps.

Using bows and arrows, which could be fired more accurately than guns from a galloping horse, Native hunters could kill a full-grown buffalo with a single shot just below the last rib.

Shocked at the slaughter, many people tried to stop buffalo hunting. But General William Sherman, the commanding general of the U.S. Army, actually encouraged overhunting as a way of destroying the Natives' food supply and starving the tribes into submission.

Plate 6 from *Catlin's North American Indian Portfolio* by George Catlin

Ho for California!

Gold! Sailors jumped ship in San Francisco to claim it. Peasants from China endured weeks of terrible travel to mine it. Europeans battled seasickness crossing the Atlantic and malaria crossing Panama to reach it. They all joined pioneers who had trudged across the Great Plains to search for riches in California. In just a few years, they turned the state from an isolated outpost into the center of the world.

IN 1848, CARPENTER JAMES Marshall found a few glittery flakes near a sawmill he was building at Coloma, California. Within four years of his discovery, 100,000 miners were swarming the California hills with dreams of getting rich picking up the yellow flakes. They relished stories of people discovering gobs of gold under their cabins...of a girl finding a "pretty rock" that turned out to be a giant gold nugget...of mourners spotting gold in a grave—and stopping the funeral until they gathered it. The dreamers figured their turn would be next.

Despite these amazing but true tales, most miners had trouble even finding the spoonful of gold a day needed to keep them in food. They suffered from scurvy because they couldn't afford to buy enough fruits and vegetables, and lived mainly on pancakes and beans.

The miners also had to be ever watchful. Although camps laid down rules governing claims, miners dared not leave their digs for fear someone would "jump"—or steal—their claim. Fights often broke out over the rights to seek gold.

Yet the miners kept searching frantically. When one dig petered out, they rushed on to find another. Some miners slept in tents, others in the open. Still others hacked down trees and threw together crude shelters in a day and a half.

Not all fortune seekers were welcome. Many of the American gold miners shouted, "California for the Americans." They bullied foreigners, especially those speaking Chinese and Spanish—even burning their camps to keep them from prospecting the best claims. But none were treated as badly as America's own Native people, who could be killed—legally—for any reason.

California was only the first of the gold rushes. By the end of the century, miners had combed the mountains from Yukon to Mexico searching for "mother lodes," main sources of the gold carried by rivers. Each new discovery brought in another flood of miners, followed by saloonkeepers, gamblers, doctors, and merchants. And in the process they helped to build up the West.

Between 1848 and 1855, miners hauled about $350 million worth of gold from California—$81 million worth in 1852 alone.

Oscar Berninghaus, *The Forty-Niners*, n.d.

American and French miners settled one dispute over a claim with a boxing match. The Americans won, but the French moved on to find an even richer strike.

Panning for gold near Denver, Colorado

Many Chinese workers came to California to seek gold. Although they were forced to work claims cleaned out by other miners, they found enough gold to live. Some also took in laundry and did other jobs that Americans didn't want.

Miners bringing gold dust to the bank, from *Harper's Weekly*, 1866

Currier & Ives, *Gold Mining in California*

Boomtowns and Entrepreneurs

Ships heavy with goods and passengers jostled for space in the sun-drenched bay while 25,000 people crowded the streets of bustling San Francisco. Thousands more stopped briefly in the city on their way to gold mines and other towns. No longer the sleepy port of Yerba Buena that it was, the San Francisco of 1849 rivaled New York as an important business center.

OTHER CITIES IN California boomed, too. Sacramento sprang up quickly in the center of the gold fields, housing 12,000 people. Many more lived in tents and wagons just outside the city, which became the new state capital.

Miners flooded into both San Francisco and Sacramento to get supplies. Soon, the merchants selling the goods became richer than the miners. One entrepreneur, Sam Brannan, became California's first millionaire by marketing picks, shovels, and gold pans. He stockpiled mining equipment, then fanned the rush for gold by running through the streets of San Francisco shouting, "Gold! Gold! Gold on the American River!" Excited Californians responded to his cry and bought their goods from him, despite his shocking prices. Even gold pans—worth only 20 cents at the time—went for $15!

Other entrepreneurs soon discovered they, too, could make money selling goods to miners. A tailor named Levi Strauss came to sell wagon covers and tents, but couldn't find enough buyers. Instead, he used the canvas cloth to make sturdy pants, which the miners loved. The pants were a hit because they lasted so long, but they were too stiff to be comfortable. Strauss later switched to denim cloth, called *genes* in France. The wildly popular pants came to be known as "jeans."

Two Eastern businessmen, Henry Wells and William Fargo, recognized the need for a safe, reliable system to transport gold to markets. They built especially strong boxes to carry the valuable metal on their stagecoaches. In addition to gold, their coaches carried passengers as well as mail, fine wines, and anything else of value. Soon their business—Wells, Fargo and Company—became the most trusted name in the West. Miners swore "by God and by Wells, Fargo." Eventually, Henry Wells and William Fargo operated most of the stagecoach lines west of the Mississippi River.

These success stories lured even more people to the West. They wanted to be there at the start of the next boom so that they, too, could make a quick buck. The entrepreneurs invested money in gold mines in Colorado, cattle in Texas, and timber in Washington. Some reaped fortunes, others lost everything they had, but they all were willing to take the risk.

Clay Street, San Francisco, 1860

From 1860 to 1863, Clark, Gruber and Company, a private banking company, minted gold coins in denominations of $2.50, $5, $10, and $20 from dust brought in by miners. The U.S. Mint took over their equipment and building in 1863.

A Wells Fargo Express wagon carrying guards and $250,000 in gold bullion, 1890

Goldhill, Nevada, ca. 1867-68

Bob Wright became the richest man in Dodge City, Kansas, by selling supplies to cowboys during cattle drives, and trading in buffalo hides. In one winter alone, he traded 200,000 hides.

In 1859, the discovery of gold at Pike's Peak near Denver, Colorado, turned a collection of 20 cabins into a major city. About 100,000 miners streamed in, many with "Pike's Peak or Bust" painted on their wagons.

Vigilantes

In 1851, an Australian drifter called Simpton stole a safe from a San Francisco merchant. He dumped it in a boat and rowed off into the bay. Alert citizens caught him, but didn't call the police. Instead, they turned Simpton over to the "vigilance committee," a group of merchants who were angry because they didn't believe the police protected them well enough. Robberies, arsons, and murders had plagued the city. The committee set up its own jury and found Simpton guilty. During the so-called trial, the vigilantes locked out the police, who had come to arrest the accused. Later, they hanged the robber in the street.

DURING THE BOOM YEARS OF the gold rush, two murders occurred every day in San Francisco alone. Vengeful citizens often meted out their own punishments. Their actions were not only illegal, but often brutal.

In smaller towns and camps that were beyond the reach of lawmen and had no courts or jails to turn to, people developed and enforced their own laws. When someone broke a law, vigilantes hastily set up a temporary court and appointed a judge for the day. These townspeople counted on the belief that quick, harsh punishments would show criminals that they would suffer if they committed crimes. They held hangings—mostly under the cover of darkness—for major crimes and dealt out whippings and fines for minor ones.

Where there *were* jails, criminals sometimes had to wait months before a judge came to town to try them. Some impatient citizens formed mobs that broke into cells, seized the prisoners, and hanged

them. In Bisbee, Arizona, one mob even disagreed with a judge's decision and hanged a man who had been sentenced to prison.

Many towns had "hanging trees" where vigilance committees strung up their victims. Bodies would dangle from the trees overnight. On their backs would be pinned notes reading "Robber," "Road Agent," or "Horse Thief."

In Bannack, Montana, in 1864, vigilantes even hanged three lawmen—Sheriff Plummer and his two deputies—who were believed to be involved in crimes. The vigilantes didn't give the accused any form of trial. What's more, they hunted down others assumed to be helping Plummer. By the time the vigilantes finished their killing spree, they had hanged 22 people whose crimes were never proven.

The only woman ever hanged by vigilantes in California was accused of murdering a drunken gambler who had broken down her door. She stabbed him the next day when he came to apologize.

The lynching of Sanford Duggan in Denver, Colorado; photographers fight for a view of the remains

An 1856 letter from the vigilance committee stating that John Stephens can leave town on the condition that he never return, "under the penalty of *death.*"

Between 1866 and 1870, vigilantes strung up 50 victims from the hanging tree in Helena, Montana. Some vigilantes would hang a thief for stealing as little as $100.

Judge David Terry stabbing a vigilance committee member, San Francisco, 1856

Hangtown (now called Placerville), California, got its name after vigilantes whipped and hanged three alleged criminals. The men couldn't defend themselves: they were too weak from the whippings and couldn't speak any English.

Two men "rescued from the authorities" and hanged by the vigilance committee, San Francisco, 1851

The Cavalry

Early one morning, Major Sandy Forsyth was jolted awake. Camped on a small island in the Republican River, Colorado, he had heard someone prowling around the horses. He called to his men. Soon after, 600 braves from the tribes that the troops had been following came whooping across the river, surrounding him and his band of 30 Cavalrymen—mounted soldiers of the U.S. Army. The braves tried to stampede the horses. When that didn't work, they slaughtered the animals, stranding the soldiers.

USING REPEATING RIFLES, Forsyth's men managed to keep the warriors at bay. On the eighth day of the siege, the air rang with the sound of bugles. The Natives knew what that meant and vanished. The Cavalry had come to the rescue.

After the American Civil War, the United States Army kept a force of about 25,000 men in the West to protect settlers and calm Natives upset by settlers taking their lands. Scattered among 100 forts, the soldiers lived in isolation and constant fear of the tribes. Stories of warriors torturing and mutilating captives ran wild. Even if the stories weren't always true, most soldiers would rather kill themselves than be captured.

Some of the men in the Cavalry were veterans of the Civil War, but most were volunteers who had simply sought a better life in the West. Few of them were prepared for the life they had to lead.

None of the forts provided good quarters for the Cavalry. Often living only in tents, soldiers endured winter cold of −35°C (−30°F) and summer heat of 38°C (100°F). Poor supplies meant they sometimes had to tolerate maggot-infested food. Unable to endure the grueling conditions, many young soldiers abandoned their posts.

Still, the men had crucial jobs to do. Besides making the country safe for settlers, they guarded railroad crews, searched the badlands for desperadoes, built roads, and mapped the country. And they became well known for their battles with the Natives.

The commanding officer in the West, General Philip Sheridan, developed a special—but cruel—tactic for attacking tribes. He ordered soldiers to strike during winter, when the Natives were least able to defend their camps. At that time of year, families were

General George Custer

short of food for themselves and their animals.

In late November 1868, General George Custer applied this tactic in a predawn raid on a Cheyenne camp in Colorado. His forces killed 101 people—mostly women and children—just as they were waking up. He destroyed any food, horses, and guns that he found and drove survivors away on foot, even though the camp's Chief Black Kettle was flying a flag of truce from his tipi.

The Cavalry sometimes used Native warriors to act as scouts against their traditional enemies and even their own people. Tribes such as the Apaches consisted of several bands, and warriors from one band were willing to scout against other bands.

Frederic Remington, *On the Southern Plains in 1860*, from *Collier's Weekly*, 1909

A buffalo soldier corporal, Pine Ridge Agency, South Dakota, 1891

Frederic Remington, *Captured*, 1899

African-American regiments made up one-fifth of the army's forces in the West. They were known as buffalo soldiers.

Not all tribes fought with the settlers. Some tribes, such as the Pawnees and Crows, accepted that they could not stop the flow of Americans and moved to reservations peacefully.

Indian Wars

Along a ridge above Pyramid Lake, Nevada, Chief Numaga and his Paiute warriors waited on horseback—close enough for the enemy to see but too far away to shoot. They simply watched as a horde of tired troopers pushed their horses through swampy meadows and up a steep trail to attack them. By the time Major Ormsby's army of volunteer soldiers reached the ridge, the Native horsemen had vanished.

SUDDENLY, EVERY CLUMP of sagebrush came alive as the warriors hidden behind them attacked. And from out of nowhere, mounted fighters whooped and charged. The panic-stricken soldiers quickly realized the trap and retreated in chaos.

Throughout the West, there were many clashes between the Native people and the soldiers. The Natives were desperate to keep their traditional way of life, living off the land they knew as their own. The soldiers believed that the land belonged to the United States and that they had every right to protect it.

No wonder there were wars. At first, pioneers negotiated with tribes only for the right to cross Native territory. But as more people moved west to claim land, they demanded that the Native people be restricted to reservations—parcels of land "reserved" for them.

Sometimes, even that wasn't enough. When miners found gold on Sioux land in South Dakota in 1874, they didn't respect the boundaries of the reservation—nor the Sioux belief that the land was sacred. The miners pressured the federal government to buy back the land, but the Native people refused to sell, setting off the Sioux Wars. Two years later, the warriors won a major victory, defeating famous "Indian fighter" General George Custer at the Battle of the Little Bighorn. They killed him and all of his troops.

Despite such successes in battle, there was no way that the Native people could win the Indian Wars overall. Their traditional style of fighting—attacking their enemies and then retreating—didn't work well against the U.S. Army. The tribes were nomadic and didn't have a way to control any land they had won. But their enemies did. The army could bring in soldiers and supplies whenever and wherever they needed them.

As the Native bands scattered across the plains after each battle, the soldiers hunted them down. Although the tribes knew the land well, their knowledge was no match for the army's persistent attacks, and in the end, they were forced onto reservations—their traditional way of life gone forever.

Sitting Bull

The Cavalry chased Sioux chief Sitting Bull over the "Medicine Line" (the U.S.-Canada border), and he and his people lived in Canada for four years. But there were few buffalo left and no land available, so Sitting Bull surrendered to the Cavalry in Montana in 1881.

Charles M. Russell, *War Council on the Plains*, 1896

Many warriors scalped their victims by cutting around the hairline and yanking off the hair with the skin still attached. They believed it was a way of taking the person's spirit. The dried scalp became a trophy of war.

Two Sioux men pose in front of a wagon after the Battle of Wounded Knee

In December 1890, while soldiers were disarming a band of captured Sioux on the way to prison, one of the braves fired a gun in the air. The soldiers panicked, killing 180 unarmed men, women, and children. Known as the Battle of Wounded Knee, the massacre was the last major battle with the Natives.

Frederic Remington, *Custer's Last Battle, Unhorsed*, 1892

Railroads

From the top of a cliff 600 meters (2,000 feet) high along the American River, California, railroad crews lowered fearless Chinese workers in wicker baskets. Clinging to the rock face, the workers pounded holes with sledges and hand drills, packed them with black powder, lit fuses, and then signaled to be hauled up. The blasts sent rock cascading to the river below, creating a narrow ledge.

THESE HARD-WORKING MEN were one of many crews doing the "impossible." They were building a railroad that would cover 3,200 kilometers (2,000 miles) through steep mountains, over high deserts, and across endless plains to link the State of California with the eastern United States.

When the railroad was completed in 1869, fantasy became reality. A six-month journey between Omaha and Sacramento by wagon train took only four days by the Iron Horse. Instead of bumping along a rough road, train passengers enjoyed the comforts of soft, upholstered seats. First-class passengers relaxed in Pullman cars with seats that converted to beds at night. Rather than cooking meals on the open prairie, any passenger could grab meals at stations along the way. For an extra fee, they could eat in a luxury dining car on the Pullman Hotel Express, which made the journey once a week.

The railroad was an immediate success. In its first year of operation, trains carried thousands of people to the West. About 230 stations popped up along the tracks. Soon new lines were developed, creating even more towns and bringing more farmers, ranchers, and miners. Settlers rushed in to take advantage of free or inexpensive land along the route. Railroad companies even sent agents to Europe to attract migrants—more people to settle along their routes. Trains heading the other direction carried goods, minerals, cattle, and grain to the eastern markets.

Unfortunately, outlaws also noticed the success of the railroad, which shipped payrolls for many companies. Robbers once held up a Central Pacific train twice on the same day. To catch thieves, railroad companies hired the Pinkerton Detective Agency—the first private detective agency in the United States—whose determined agents spread across the West, searching for gangs.

To the Native peoples, the railroads spelled disaster. The tracks ignored their traditional lands— even their reservations—and disrupted their buffalo hunting. Days after the last spike completed the transcontinental railroad, Cheyenne warriors tore up the track at Fossil Creek, Kansas. Despite their efforts and those of other tribes, the railroad stayed and flourished.

William Thompson and his crew of five men rode in a hand car from Plum Creek, Nebraska, and hit a barricade Cheyenne warriors had set up across the tracks. The warriors killed the crew and scalped the unconscious Thompson, who later found his scalp and crawled back to town. Doctors saved Thompson's life, but weren't able to reattach his hair.

Workers pose on a pony engine during the construction of the Union Pacific Railroad

Gamblers found the trains a good spot to ply their trade. With a bible and a big gun, well-known card shark "Poker" Alice Ivers rode many trains looking for a game.

Poker Alice

Detective Allen Pinkerton and his men, 1862

A railroad workers' camp near Humboldt River Canyon, Nevada

To create the transcontinental railroad, two companies—Union Pacific and Central Pacific—worked from opposite ends, one heading west and the other heading east. The tracks met in Promontory, Utah.

Joining the tracks for the first transcontinental railroad

At the Ranch

"Come on boys, get up!" the cook would shout at 3:30 in the morning. The cowboys rose quickly—at the spring roundup they knew they wouldn't get much sleep for a few weeks. Over the winter, the cattle had scattered far and wide over the open range. Cowboys from many different ranches joined forces to find them. They would be living in a moving camp until they had searched every nook and cranny of the range.

RIDING OUT IN ALL DIRECTIONS, they formed broad circles—as large as 32 kilometers (20 miles) in diameter—around each of the camps. As the sun came up, they zigzagged slowly back to the center, chasing any cattle they found ahead of them. They roped cows that tried to escape their circle and drove them into one large herd.

Next, the cowboys sorted the herd by riding among the cattle, checking the brands that had been burned into their rumps. They separated the cows belonging to their ranch from the rest of the herd. Cowboys used specially trained "cutting" horses to separate the calves from their mothers. Once the calves were cut from the herd, they were branded. Three men held the bawling calf down while a fourth pulled a hot branding iron out of the fire and pressed it against the animal's hide.

Unmarked strays, called mavericks, were also separated from the herd and branded. In the late 1860s, as many as 5 million of these mavericks roamed the grasslands. They were claimed by whichever ranches rounded them up.

The cowboys also captured any wild mustangs they found and tamed them for ranch work. It took courage and persistence. The cowboys eased onto the horses, then hung on tight while the broncos bucked furiously. If they were tossed off, the cowboys got right back on until the animals were "broken" and accepted them as masters.

All of these jobs required stamina. Spending 12 hours a day in the saddle, cowboys had to be expert horsemen and skilled ropers to control the herds. They honed skills passed on from the Mexican *vaqueros*, who had been raising cattle on the open range since the 16th century.

But being a cowboy wasn't all work. At the roundups, they were eager to show off their skills in friendly competitions to win bragging rights. They competed to see who could rope a steer the fastest and who could stay on a bucking bronco the longest. They gambled to see who would have to ride the wildest horse or steer. Soon the competitions between ranches drew audiences, and cowboys, who normally never wore belts, competed for silver belt buckles— awards that recognized their special skills on the range.

Roundup on Sherman Ranch, Kansas

A cowboy seldom had a horse of his own. Instead, he rode the mount provided by the ranch. If he did own a horse, he would add it to the ranch's herd as a symbol of his commitment to his employer.

Charles M. Russell, *The Bucking Bronco*

The cowboys developed their own lingo from the Spanish words of the Mexicans. *Vaquero* became buckaroo, *rancho* became ranch, *chaparreras* became chaps, *la reata* became lariat, and *bronco caballo* became bronco. Rodeo and corral are the same in both languages.

An African-American cowboy and his horse.

Although movies today portray cowboys as mostly English-speaking, white Americans, about one in seven were Spanish-speaking Mexicans and almost as many others were African Americans.

Mealtime at the camp, Birdwood Ranch, Nebraska

On the Trail

Lightning pierced the night sky. Thunder deafened the cowboys. All of a sudden, a frightened herd of bawling cattle charged across the prairie. The cowboys spurred their horses to get ahead of the stampede. Trying desperately to turn the herd, the cowboys shot at the horns of the lead cows so they would change direction and start to run in a circle. It took a great deal of skill and bravery to slow the momentum of thousands of charging cattle.

STAMPEDES WERE ONLY ONE OF the dangers that cowboys faced on cattle drives. Most of the problems were natural ones—extreme drought, widespread grass fires, foaming rivers. When normally calm waters became swollen torrents, the cattle often panicked. Spurring their horses into the rushing water, the cowboys worked fast to get the cows to shore before they drowned.

To protect their cattle, ranchers hired one cowboy for every 250 cows. On the drive, the trail boss always rode in front of the closely packed herd. Flank riders stayed along the sides to prevent the animals from straying. Drag riders followed behind, prodding any stragglers. A "wrangler" cared for the horses so the cowboys could always have fresh mounts. But after the trail boss, the most important man was always the cook, who looked after bedrolls and medicine as well as the food.

Cattle drives started after the American Civil War when the demand for beef soared and there was a lot of money to be made. Herds sold in Kansas for more than 10 times their value in Texas, where there were no railroads to get them to Eastern markets.

Cowboys first used the "Old Chisholm Trail," a wagon route made by trader Jesse Chisholm, to bring cattle from as far away as San Antonio, Texas, to Abilene, Kansas. Later, they used other trails, including the Western Trail to Dodge City, Kansas, and the Goodnight-Loving Trail to Denver, Colorado, and Cheyenne, Wyoming.

As soon as the grass turned green in the early spring, the cowboys headed out. For three to four months, they spent 12 hours a day in the saddle, breathing the dust kicked up by the cattle. They lived on beef stew, beans, and biscuits, and tolerated coffee "hot as hell, black as sin, and strong as death" because it masked the taste of the bad water along the trail. And every night they slept under the open sky.

Despite the hard work and low pay, these "knights of the plains" enjoyed respect for their courage and endurance. They lived by a code of honor that valued loyalty, respect, and independence.

Charles M. Russell, *Cowpunching Sometimes Spells Trouble*, 1889

At night the cowboys sang songs around campfires to calm the cattle as well as entertain themselves.

Rounding up the herd, 1887

Cowboys spent a lot of money on handmade boots that were designed for riding—not walking. Thin soles allowed them to feel the stirrups and high heels prevented their feet from sliding forward.

A Texas cattle drive

A cowboy's most important possession was his saddle. The saying, "He's sold his saddle," meant that the cowboy was broke.

Range Wars

Snow greeted 50 hired gunmen—"regulators"—as they poured off the train in Casper, Wyoming, in 1892. But even colder was the reason they had come. A group of land-rich ranchers had hired them to kill men accused of stealing cattle. The gunmen stopped at a small ranch owned by Nate Champion. Even against so many gunfighters, Nate defended himself for most of a day until the regulators burned down his house and shot him—28 times! A few days later, the Cavalry captured the regulators to stop the killing.

THE ISSUE? WHO CONTROLLED the rights to the grasslands. The government owned most of the land, but ranchers grazed their cattle on public land as well as their own ranches. Some ranchers believed that, because they arrived first, the grasslands and the mavericks belonged to them. They thought they had the right to drive away competitors, particularly farmers and sheepherders. But in fact, everybody had rights to the land. The government even encouraged homesteaders to settle by offering free land to those willing to farm it.

Still, ranchers battled settlers who tried to claim the grasslands, particularly if anything interfered with the cattle getting to water. The ranchers cut barbed-wire fences around homesteads and let their animals trample the farmers' crops. Some built their own fences on the open ranges just to block homesteaders' routes to town, and shot at anyone trying to cut through. Other ranchers had their employees file false homestead claims, keeping the most important lands for cattle. Yet despite the range wars, the homesteaders kept coming, squeezing the cattlemen onto smaller parcels of public land. The ranchers couldn't stop the flood.

To discourage sheepherders, ranchers declared "deadlines." They set up borders and decreed that no one could bring sheep across them—under threat of death. Some ranchers would poison sheep, club them, or drive them off cliffs. In 1884, one gang of ranchers killed 4,000 sheep by herding them into quicksand along the Little Colorado River, Arizona.

Overgrazing finally forced ranchers into managing their herds better. Instead of depending on public land, they bought more range land, pumped in water, and raised hay to feed cattle. These changes gradually brought an end to the range wars and peace to the grasslands.

In 1874, Joseph Glidden invented barbed wire to create the first inexpensive way to fence ranges and farmland. It was an instant success.

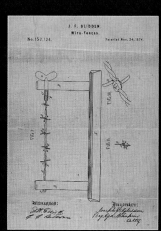

The patent drawing for Joseph Glidden's Improvement to Barbed Wire, 1874

Frederic Remington, *Arresting Cattle Thieves*

The bloodiest range war of any in the West, the Graham-Tewksbury feud, was a battle between two large families of cattle ranchers. For six years, the two families fought each other until 25 men lay dead. Only one person survived—a Tewksbury.

Holding down a lot in Guthrie, Oklahoma Territory, 1889

The land office in Round Pond, Oklahoma Territory, 1894

The Wyoming Cattle Growers Association hired former army scout and detective Tom Horner to kill alleged rustlers. But the long-distance marksman was hanged for killing a 14-year-old boy by mistake.

Out on the Town

After three or four months in the saddle, eating dust along the trail, cowboys were desperate for a wild night on the town. Money jingled in their pockets, and there was plenty of time to cut loose and have some fun. But first things first. The men headed straight for clothing stores to buy everything from socks and underwear to bandannas and hats. Outfits worn day and night on cattle drives were so filthy and smelly they had to be burned.

SECOND STOP WAS THE barbershop. After haircuts and hot baths—taken in metal tubs in back rooms—the cowboys started to feel human again. Cleaned and dressed in their brand-new duds, they strutted into photography studios for souvenir pictures to send home.

Then, they really whooped it up. They rode around town yelling and shooting their guns. They even ran their horses down the wooden sidewalks or right through the swinging doors of the saloons. A favorite "sport" was shooting at the feet of innocent townspeople to make them dance.

Final destination, the saloons: wild places where the cowboys bought their favorite beverage, whiskey. Most saloons were just plain barrooms with sawdust-covered floors that soaked up stray spit from drinkers who chewed tobacco. Larger ones offered all kinds of

Saloons and disreputable places of Hazen, Nevada

entertainment that could provide the cowpokes with some fun, including billiards tables, poker games, and cancan girls.

The saloons were crowded from early morning until late at night. The cowboys were joined by miners, soldiers, railroaders, and buffalo hunters who were just as ready for a good time. It was not unusual for a man to drink a whole bottle of whiskey in a day. And fights were frequent. Their wild times left the men suffering with throbbing heads and bruise-covered bodies. Now and

then, one of the brawlers even ended up dead!

Many townspeople wanted to set aside saloon areas in their communities as special "cowboy sections," and some of them did. As soon as the cowboys headed back to Texas in late summer, saloons in these sections would close. Life would quiet down—until the next cattle drive rolled in with another lot of lonely men looking for recreation and entertainment.

Before the railroads arrived, whiskey was hard to get in the West, so saloonkeepers sold pure alcohol. They diluted it with water, flavored it with coffee, and spiced it up with pepper. The men called it "rotgut" because it was so hard on their stomachs.

Saloon patrons, Turret, Colorado

During construction of the Union Pacific Railroad, temporary saloons and gambling halls sprang up at the end of the line. These "Hells on Wheels" just shifted location as the tracklayers moved west.

Charles M. Russell, *Utica [A Quiet Day in Utica]*, 1907

Cowboys worked as a team on the trail, but split up in town because the Mexican and African-American cowboys usually had to drink at bars apart from the whites.

Gamblers and Dance-hall Girls

One morning, a man in Denver, Colorado, was waiting impatiently for the bank to open. As soon as it did, he rushed in, begging for a $5,000 loan and produced five cards—four kings and an ace—as a guarantee. The teller refused his request, but the bank manager ordered him to give the gambler the loan. Just ten minutes later, the man returned with the $5,000, plus $500 interest from the pot he had just won at poker. The manager said the bank would always risk its money on a winning hand.

THIS TALL TALE WAS A popular joke in the 1870s, but high-stakes gambling was not. Many people gambled to ease their boredom or loneliness. Betting on cards entertained players for a full day—or until their money was gone. They were willing to risk everything they had on the turn of a single card. Saloons often hired professional gamblers to attract customers. Good gamblers made big bucks—and not just for themselves.

Not all gamblers relied on skill. Slick ones had many devious ways of cheating. Some companies sold marked card decks so that players could tell what their opponents had in their hand. Professionals preferred to mark their own decks by adding ink dots to the backs, making pinholes that they could feel, or cutting the corners slightly. Others cheated by having partners look on and signal what was in an opponent's hand. Although many gamblers were aware that cheating was common, they were still willing to get into a game, especially poker.

If there was a dance hall attached to a saloon, lonely men happily paid for opportunities to dance with "hurdy-girls," mostly unmarried women hired for the job. Their name came from the hurdy-gurdy, a crank-operated instrument that some saloons used to make music. The men stomped their boots and waved their hats in the air, while the women twirled their skirts.

Between dances, the hurdy-girls encouraged their partners to buy liquor. While the men drank whiskey, the women sipped cold tea to stay sober. They earned a portion of the liquor sales as well as money from the dancing. They also guided their drunken partners to gambling tables.

In the bigger saloons, entertainers performed on stage. Often a line of dance-hall girls did the high-kicking "cancan." With skirts raised high and legs swinging, they showed off layers of brightly colored petticoats, mesh stockings, and frilly underwear. Traveling comedians did stand-up routines, and singers belted out the latest ballads. All were encouraging the cowboys to spend their meager wages.

A Faro game in full blast at the Orient Saloon, Bisbee, Arizona

Gamblers bet on dice as well as cards. Sometimes they loaded the dice, weighting them so that certain numbers came up more often.

Gamblers risked their lives if they called their opponents cheaters. Many card players carried derringers, small but deadly guns, in their pockets, and they weren't afraid to use them.

A lively night at the dance hall

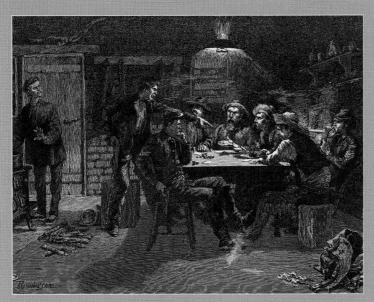

Frederic Remington, *A Quarrel, Over Cards*, from *Harper's Weekly*, 1887

Crapper Jack's Saloon, Cripple Creek, Colorado

Famed gunman and gambler Wild Bill Hickok was shot in the back of the head while playing poker in Deadwood, South Dakota in 1876. At the time, he held two black eights and two black aces, which became known as "dead man's hand."

Frontier Towns

As winds fanned the flames, everybody in town helped the fire brigade. The hoses from the hand pump weren't quite long enough to control the blaze, so people resorted to using buckets of water, wet gunnysacks, and shovels. A line formed quickly to pass water from the cistern to the fire. Despite everyone's hard work, many buildings were lost and the townspeople had to start rebuilding their homes and businesses from scratch the next day.

SCENES LIKE THIS ONE unfolded in many small towns, where people often struggled with disasters. Fires swept through wooden buildings, spring thaws sent water coursing down muddy streets, fierce winds blew the roofs off houses, and blizzards forced people to dig tunnels through snowdrifts just to get out of their homes.

Frontier towns usually started out as clusters of crude, temporary huts. Residents would just pick up and move closer to the growing railroad or the latest gold strike. Four months after Garland City, Colorado was founded, innkeeper Joe Perry served his guests breakfast, loaded his inn on a railroad car, and shipped it 48 kilometers (30 miles) to Alamosa. He served supper in it there that night.

Despite such crude beginnings, the towns continued to attract people. The first permanent residents would be hotel-keepers. They catered to almost everyone who arrived to settle or was just passing through. In some cases, the hotel was only a small building where guests slept on the floor. Then a saloon would spring up next to the hotel to provide entertainment.

The hub of any town was the general store. Not only did it sell everything from groceries to saddles, and candy to plows, but it also provided a meeting place. People gathered around the store's potbellied stove to exchange the latest gossip.

Saturday was always the biggest day in town. Country folk flocked in to buy groceries and sell produce. In the evening, everyone gathered in a school or barn for the social event of the week, the dance.

Each year, the towns-people waited anxiously for the circus to arrive. They turned out first for a grand parade of bands, animal cages, and steam organs. Then they thrilled to the colorful performances of clowns, trained elephants, and trapeze artists. To add to the fun, most towns also ran local events, such as foot races and pig wrestling, while the circus was around.

By the 1890s, thousands of small towns dotted the West. Although many of them disappeared during the next century, a number prospered and grew into cities such as Denver and Kansas City.

The North Ameri[c]
Hotel, Placerville,
California

Storefronts in Corinne, Utah, 1869

Many commercial buildings were given fake fronts to make them look bigger. Some even had phony windows to create the appearance of a second story.

Traveling performers drew crowds to patent medicine salesmen, who sold bizarre concoctions "guaranteed" to cure everything that ailed everybody.

A teacher and her students in front of a sod schoolhouse, Oklahoma Territory, 1895

The first public buildings erected were usually schools—often log cabins, sod huts, or sheds. The students were expected to chop wood for the stove, haul water, and shovel snow.

Deadwood, Dakota Territory, 1876

Wearing the Badge

One fall evening in 1871, Marshal Wild Bill Hickok heard shooting in front of the Alamo Saloon in Abilene, Kansas. With guns drawn, he raced to the scene and exchanged gunfire with a partying cowboy named Phil Coe. During the shootout, a bullet tore Hickok's coat, but one of the marshal's shots was right on target. He hit Coe in the stomach and killed him. Still on guard, Hickok heard footsteps behind him, turned fast, and fired at the approaching figure. Deputy Mike Williams, who had been running to his aid, fell dead.

LIKE MANY LAWMEN IN the West, Wild Bill Hickok had earned a reputation as a tough gunfighter, or "shootist," even before he got the job of marshal. He could hit the center of a target every time, and he was known for his brave exploits during the Civil War. He was the perfect man, the city council thought, to control violence on the streets.

In the wild West, it was hard to tell the good guys from the bad. Many shootists changed sides on a whim: outlaws became lawmen—and lawmen became outlaws. Notorious gunslinger Ben Thompson admitted that he had killed 32 men before he was elected city marshal of Austin, Texas. Deputies Grat and Bob Dalton in Indian Territory, later called Oklahoma, found enforcing the law was too much work and turned to robbery as an easier way to make a buck.

James Butler (Wild Bill) Hickok

Whatever their beginnings, lawmen were deadly in carrying out their duties. In 1881, Marshal Virgil Earp of Tombstone, Arizona, along with his brothers, Wyatt and Morgan, and their friend, Doc Holliday, quarreled with four suspected cattle rustlers. When Marshal Earp demanded the men hand over their weapons, a gunfight broke out. In 30 seconds, three of the suspected rustlers lay bleeding in the street behind a horse corral. The battle, called the Gunfight at the OK Corral, became the most famous shootout in the history of the West. Because two of the suspects had been unarmed, Wyatt Earp and Doc Holliday were charged with murder, but a judge ruled that the shootings were self-defense.

Many lawmen mastered the "quick draw." But, unlike the sheriffs in movies today, they never entered face-to-face duels with their guns still in their holsters. That would have given their opponents a head start of a fraction of a second. In reality, shootists whipped out their guns before trouble started. They lived by the principle, "Shoot first, ask questions later."

Wearing the badge made heroes of some of the toughest men in the West. They put their lives on the line every time they came up against ruthless outlaws. And their daring exploits made them legends.

Dodge City Peace Commissioners, left to right:
Chas. Bassett, W. H. Harris, Wyatt Earp, Luke Short,
L. McLean, Bat Masterson, and Neal Brown

A wooden jailhouse

Sheriff Bat Masterson of Dodge City, Kansas, gained a reputation for keeping cowboys in line by batting them on the head with his cane. But everyone knew how good he was with his guns.

Wyatt Earp, the famous gunfighter and marshal of Dodge City, started his "career" throughout the West as a horse thief and gambler. Earlier, he had been fired as a policeman in Wichita for pocketing the fines he had collected.

Charles M. Russell, *The Call of the Law*

A marshal was like the "chief of police" in a town and had deputies working under him to uphold the law. A sheriff was responsible for keeping the law in an entire county, which included several towns. When needed, he gathered ordinary citizens to form posses to hunt for outlaws.

Gangs of the West

In February 1866, 12 tough men rode their horses into Liberty, Missouri. Ten of them stood guard outside the Clay County Savings Association while two others pulled on masks and stole $60,000 from the bank—a huge haul considering that cowboys of the day worked for $25 a month. As the gang galloped out of town, they shot an innocent bystander, adding murder to their crime. Later that night, they escaped a 30-man sheriff's posse who pursued them through a blinding snowstorm. Gang leaders Jesse and Frank James instantly nabbed newspaper headlines. Over the next 15 years, they continued their crime spree, stealing an estimated $175,000 in all.

AFTER THE AMERICAN Civil War, many soldiers, such as the James brothers, had found it hard to return to their former lives. They applied their riding and shooting skills to robbing banks and trains, particularly targeting companies that had supported their wartime enemies in the North.

On July 21, 1873, in Adair County, Iowa, the James brothers, with a group of outlaws called the Younger gang, pulled railroad tracks apart as the Rock Island train approached. The engine overturned, killing the engineer. Then seven masked men, shooting and yelling, entered the baggage car and emptied two safes of $2,000—far less than the $100,000 shipment of gold they had expected. Still, they are remembered for being the first to rob a train in the West.

Other thieves imitated the James and Younger gangs. In Coffeyville, Kansas, in 1892, five members of another outlaw gang, the Dalton brothers, wanted to outdo their idols by robbing two banks at the same time. The townspeople caught on when the gang appeared wearing obviously fake whiskers. As the thieves entered the banks—two in one and three in the other—the citizens armed themselves. Bullets flew in all directions as the outlaws left the banks. After 12 minutes of fighting, four of the robbers and four of the townspeople lay dead, but the citizens had saved the loot!

Despite constant bloodshed, gangs continued to form. Shortly after the last shot was fired in the Coffeyville robbery, Bill Doolin, one of the Dalton gang members, formed the Wild Bunch. They terrorized the Oklahoma Territory for the next three years. Butch Cassidy headed another fast-shooting, bank-robbing gang, also called the Wild Bunch, out of Hole in the Wall, Wyoming, a famous mountain hideout.

But new technology made old-style robbing more difficult. While the James gang could evade posses sent to chase them, later gangs had trouble outriding the telegraph and the telephone lines. Marshals could just call ahead to lawmen in neighboring towns to capture criminals. And they did.

The stories told by Bill Doolin's Wild Bunch inspired two teenage girls, Little Britches and Cattle Annie, to act as spies for the gang. The girls also stole horses and traded whiskey on their own before the law caught up with them.

Charles M. Russell, *The Hold Up*

In 1882, Jesse James lived in St. Joseph, Missouri, under the name of Thomas Howard. Gang member Bob Ford shot and killed the unarmed Jesse in his home when he turned his back to straighten a picture. Ford became known as the "coward who shot Mr. Howard."

The Hole in the Wall Gang: Harry Longabaugh (The Sundance Kid), Will Carver, Ben Kilpatrick, Harvey Logan (Kid Curry), and Robert Leroy Parker (Butch Cassidy)

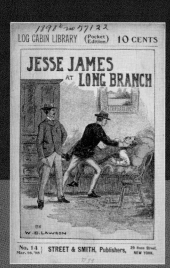

Jesse James at Long Branch, an 1898 dime novel

Belle Starr, in *The National Police Gazette*, 1886

"Bandit Queen" Belle Starr of Youngers Bend, Indian Territory, was a friend of the James brothers and Cole Younger. Although she was only ever convicted of horse theft, she hid outlaws in her home and is believed to have masterminded many robberies.

Lone Gunmen

Angered by his neighbor's snoring, John Wesley Hardin shot through the wall of his room in the American Hotel in Abilene, Kansas. His first shot woke the snorer, his second killed him. To get out of town before Marshal Wild Bill Hickok arrived at the scene, Hardin climbed out of the window in his nightshirt and escaped on a stolen horse.

WES HARDIN, A RUTHLESS KILLER who claimed to have murdered 44 men, was the deadliest gunslinger in the West. But as fast and accurate as he was with a gun, he carefully avoided any shootout with Wild Bill Hickok. He feared the marshal might beat him to the draw.

Many lone gunmen spurned the safety of gang life. They preferred to rely on their own wits and speed. Their reputations as cold-blooded killers were their armor. Other gunmen believed it would be suicide to face them.

New Mexico's Billy the Kid became the most famous outlaw in the West. He gained his reputation as a killer at age 17 for shooting a bully who had picked on him. The Kid furthered his fame by fighting in a range war and escaping jail several times. He was caught only by a stroke of luck on the part of Sheriff Pat Garrett of Lincoln, New Mexico in 1881. The two were guests at the same ranch and neither was aware that the other was there. The sheriff recognized the Kid's voice in a dark room and shot him, killing the 21-year-old.

Not all lone outlaws killed to get what they wanted. Some of them were just wily. Black Bart, for instance, would rob a stagecoach by crouching low in front of it so the guard risked harming his own horses if he opened fire. Seeing "gun barrels" pointed at them, the driver and guard believed they were in grave danger when Bart shouted orders to his "accomplices." Authorities later learned that the supposed guns were merely sticks and that Black Bart worked alone. Still, he eluded Wells Fargo's best detective for eight years.

Mysterious loners, such as Hardin, the Kid, and Black Bart, became renowned for their daring and ruthlessness. They captured the attention of the sensation-seeking press. Even during his short life, Billy the Kid had his name emblazoned on many newspapers and books, where writers portrayed the killer as both hero and villain. Today, his name is as well known as it was over a hundred years ago.

Freelance gunmen roamed the West selling their services to stagecoach lines, railroad companies, and ranches. They would hunt and sometimes kill robbers, rustlers, and sheepherders. Ranchers gave them respectable-sounding titles such as "cattle detectives" or "stock inspectors."

William Robinson Leigh,
The Hold Up [The Ambush], 1903

Billy the Kid

With guns blazing, Pearl Hart and partner Joe Boot robbed an Arizona stagecoach in 1899 and escaped into the hills. But the inexperienced thieves got lost, so a posse had no trouble finding them a couple of days later.

Notorious outlaw Benjamin J. Hodges poses with his sawed-off shotgun

Legends of Joaquin Murieta, a bandit who robbed stagecoaches, held up saloons, and raided gold camps, flourished in California, but no one was sure if he was really one man or many.

Wanted dead or alive

REWARD
($5,000.00)

Reward for the capture, dead or alive, of one Wm. Wright, better known as

"BILLY THE KID"

Age, 18. Height, 5 feet, 3 inches. Weight, 125 lbs. Light hair, blue eyes and even features. He is the leader of the worst band of desperadoes the Territory has ever had to deal with. The above reward will be paid for his capture or positive proof of his death.

JIM DALTON, Sheriff.

DEAD OR ALIVE!
"BILLY THE KID"

Judges

When Roy Bean, owner of the Jersey Lilly Saloon in Langtry, Texas, hung up his apron and put on an old coat, his tavern became a courthouse—with his pet bear, Bruno, sitting in the corner. He hit the bar with his gun butt and exclaimed, "Hear ye! Hear ye! This court is now in session."

ONE DAY, AN IRISH RAILroad worker accused of killing a Chinese laborer faced the judge. Bean thumbed through his only law book, *The Revised Statutes of Texas,* 1879. He noted the laws against murder, but they didn't mention anything against killing a "Chinaman." To narrow-minded Bean, this meant no crime had occurred. He acquitted the man!

In many towns across the West, ordinary people became judges. Some weighed evidence in proper courthouses; others made decisions inside tents and saloons, such as Bean's Jersey Lilly. Despite their lack of legal training—and sometimes racist views— most judges made fair and common-sense rulings.

Yet many judges gained the reputation of "hanging judges." One of the most feared was a federal judge and trained lawyer named Isaac Parker, who presided over Western Arkansas District, including the Indian Territory. During his

first eight weeks on the job, he tried a huge number of cases—91—and, of the 15 men accused of murder, he sentenced 7 to death. During his 21-year career, he ordered the hangings of 160 people—though almost half later appealed his decisions in other courts and escaped the death penalty.

Judges such as Parker often handed down unreasonably harsh sentences so that other criminals would think twice before breaking any laws in their jurisdictions. In the 1870s, killings were commonplace. As many as 100 people a year were murdered in the Indian Territory alone, and many outlaws escaped justice by holing up there. No wonder the Territory was called the "Robbers' Roost."

Not only did judges in the West believe that punishment had to be harsh, they also believed it had to be public so that everyone— even children—would see the hangings. Judge Parker had his executioner, ex-lawman George

Maledon, construct huge gallows for hangings. Sometimes a crowd of 5,000 people watched the hangman spring the trapdoor, dropping a condemned man to his death. Maledon personally hanged 87 of the 88 people who couldn't escape Parker's death sentences. At times, he lined up six people on the gallows and hanged them all at once!

Although some judges made decisions that were brutal—even bizarre— their increasing presence did help tame the West. Working with other lawmen, they established a system of justice that applied to everyone.

Isaac Parker

Getting juries in less populated areas presented some difficulties. One trial was delayed three days because a judge asked a juror to wear his coat in the court. The man had to ride 130 kilometers (80 miles) to his home to get his coat.

Judge Roy Bean made some of the wackiest decisions in the West. He once fined a corpse $40, the amount found on the body, for carrying a concealed pistol.

Judge Roy Bean holding court at his saloon, trying a horse thief, Langtry, Texas, 1900

Wyoming was the first state to give women the right to vote and hold office. In 1870, Esther Morris, the first woman Justice of the Peace in the U.S., presided over 26 cases in South Pass City, Wyoming. Overall, her judgments were considered very fair.

The hanging of Gilbert and Rosengrants in Leadville, Colorado, 1881

Wild West Shows

The Deadwood Mail Coach careened down a dusty road with Buffalo Bill Cody firing his rifle. Waving tomahawks over their heads, a dozen warriors were chasing after the speeding stage. But as they leaped onto the back, Cody beat them off.

JAMMED INTO THE STANDS at the Omaha Fairgrounds, thousands of people roared, just as they had for the rest of the four-hour program of death-defying riding events, incredible shooting exhibitions, and daring re-enactments of the Indian Wars. Cody's Wild West Show of 1883 was a smash hit—an extravaganza that could only be performed in an open arena.

People throughout North America and Europe who had never seen buffalo before felt the rush of being in the middle of a hunt. Crowds who had only heard of the bravery of the Plains tribes were caught up in a savage battle. Cody did more than just satisfy their hunger for glimpses of the perils and gallantry of life on the Western frontier. He made the scenes real.

Within 10 years, more than 50 Wild West shows traveled the world, feeding the public's appetite for danger and heroism. Buffalo Bill's friend Gordon "Pawnee Bill" Lillie started

another large-scale Wild West show in 1888. The two shows joined forces in 1908 and toured as the Two Bills' Show, or Buffalo Bill's Wild West Show and Pawnee Bill's Great Far East Show.

And until it stopped touring in 1916, Cody's show was the best around. A cast of Sioux re-enacted the defeat of Custer in the Battle of the Little Bighorn. Even Sioux Chief Sitting Bull, famous for his battle victories, toured with the show for a year. Considered one of the greatest sharp-shooters the world has ever seen, Annie Oakley starred by shooting a cigarette out of her assistant's mouth or hitting the center of an ace of spades. She went as far as aiming through a

mirror at her targets over her shoulder.

In 1887, Buffalo Bill crossed the Atlantic with 97 Natives, 18 buffalo, 181 horses, 10 elk, four donkeys, five longhorns, two deer, and a concord stagecoach. Just getting to a seaport took 18 train cars. While the show was in Europe, Grand Duke Michael of Russia challenged Annie Oakley to a target shooting competition, but he was no match for her.

By bringing the West to life for audiences, the Wild West shows generated a passion for Western entertainment of all kinds. And their scenes of larger-than-life heroes and dramatic events became the stuff of legend.

A U.S. Cavalry rifle display during Buffalo Bill's Wild West Show

Prairie Rose Henderson gained fame in the Irwin Brothers Wild West Show by riding broncos. She was known for her bizarre costumes of beads, feathers, and sequins, which she made herself.

A poster for George Sanger's Great Circus and the Wild West

In June 1887, Bill Cody's Wild West Show was extremely popular in England, even performing for Queen Victoria at Windsor Castle.

A poster for Buffalo Bill's extravagant drama *The Prairie Waif*

Annie Oakley shoots targets in Buffalo Bill's Wild West Show

In 1886, Pawnee Bill married 15-year-old May Manning. She learned to ride and shoot from the Pawnee tribe living near their ranch in Kansas and became a star in her husband's show.

Epilogue

THE 1890S SAW THE END OF THE WILD, WILD WEST. By then, the untamed land that pioneers first crossed was just a memory. But the people who settled the West had certainly left their mark. Their stories were celebrated in Wild West shows and popular novels of the day, and their spirit, courage, and independence inspired the generation that followed.

Rodeos that began as simple competitions at cattle roundups became major productions. Crowds packed auditoriums at the Boston Garden and New York's Madison Square Garden to watch professional bronco busting and steer wrestling. Cowboys became celebrity rodeo performers, traveling the world to show off their skills.

Hopalong Cassidy, Tom Mix, Roy Rogers, and Gene Autry— all stars of Western films in the first half of the 20th century— shot their six-guns across the screen. Fans thrilled to frontier heroes charging after outlaws, tough gunfighters dueling in the streets, and masked gangs holding up trains. Audiences jeered the villains wearing black hats and cheered the "champions of justice" wearing white.

But it didn't stop there. In the 1950s and 1960s, western movies became more sophisticated, and stories of the old West also appeared on TV screens. Each week, viewers all over the world tuned in to programs about everything from cattle drives to gunfighters such as Wyatt Earp. One of the most popular cowboy shows, called *Bonanza,* ran for 14 years.

Today, the romance and adventure of frontier life still captivate people. Rodeos and stampedes continue to draw audiences, and Western stories thrive in books and films. Many legends overlook the hard work that went into making the West, but they do capture the enduring spirit of the settlers: people who risked everything to forge a new life in a tough land. And their tales still inspire people to conquer their own frontiers.

Soon after motion pictures were invented in 1896, Buffalo Bill Cody and his Wild West Show appeared in factual short features, but *The Great Train Robbery* (1903) was considered the first real "Western."

Tad Lucas, Champion All Round Cowgirl and World's Champion Woman Trick Rider, became the only woman to ride a wild brahma bull in Madison Square Garden, in 1925.

To control an ornery steer, rodeo star Bill Pickett jumped off his horse, grabbed the steer by its horns, and wrestled it to the ground. Then he bit the animal's lower lip, like bulldogs do to control cattle. The sport became known as bulldogging or steer wrestling.

Index

Photo Credits

Cover, i, 1, 44, based on *In Without Knocking* by Charles M. Russell, lithograph by Brown & Bigelow; **Back Cover, i, 23 upper right,** based on *The Bucking Bronco* by Charles M. Russell; **2–3 left,** *The Quarrel* by Frederic Remington; **5 lower left,** *Life on the Prairie. The Trappers Defense, "Fire Fight Fire"* by Arthur Fitzwilliam Tait, lithograph by Currier & Ives; **8–9,** *Catlin's North American Indian Portfolio* by George Catlin, plate 6; **11 lower right,** Currier & Ives, *Gold Mining in California,* lithograph; **11 lower right,** *Banking House, Denver City, Colorado—Miners Bringing in Gold Dust* by Theodore R. Davis, *Harper's Magazine;* **12–13 upper,** *Views of San Francisco,* page 44; **14–15,** *Tremendous Excitement! Samual Whittaker and Robert McKensie Rescued from the Authorities, and Hung by Vigilance Committee...* lithograph by Justh. Quirot & Co., 1851; **16–17 upper,** *On the Southern Plains in 1860* by Frederic Remington, lithograph by P.F. Collier & Son, 1909; **21 upper left,** Andrew J. Russell; **31 middle,** *Dance-House* by Henry Worrall, reproduced from Joseph G. McCoy's *Historic sketches of the cattle trade of the West and Southwest,* 1874; **31 lower left,** *A Quarrel, Over Cards—A Sketch from a New Mexican Ranch* by Frederic Remington, reproduced from Harpers Weekly, 1887; **34,** *James Butler (Wild Bill) Hickok (1817–1876),* The State Historical Society of Wisconsin; **34–35,** *The Call of the Law* by Charles M. Russell, lithograph by Brown & Bigelow, 1914; **36–37 upper,** *The Hold Up* by Charles Russell; **39 upper right,** reproduced from Emerson Hough's *The story of the outlaw ...* The Outing Publishing Company, 1907: p. 258–259; **39, lower right; 43 upper right,** *... Buffalo Bills— New Drama The Prairie Waif* by W.F. Cody and Josh E. Ogden. All courtesy Yale Collection of Western Americana, Beinecke Rare Book and Manuscript Library.

3 upper right, Northwestern Photographic Co., X-31289; **3 lower right,** Oscar William, X-21803; **7 upper left,** Alice (A.) Stewart Hill scrapbook (C MSS WH162), X-11929; **11 upper right,** Louis Charles McClure, MCC-1918A; **15 upper left,** *Lynching of Duggan in Denver fight of photographers for view of remains,* engraving by A.P. Proctor, reproduced from D.J. Cook, *Hands Up,* Z-132; **17 lower left,** Clarence Grant Morledge, X-31308; **18–19,** *Custer's last battle, unhorsed* by Frederic Remington, reproduction of a Frederic Remington magazine illustration: Cent. January 1892, X-33634; **19 upper right,** photo reproduction by A.G. Johnson, X-31487; **21 left middle,** X-22174; **23 middle right,** X-21563; **23 lower right,** X-21930; **26–27 upper,** *Arresting Cattle Thieves* by Frederic Remington, lithograph by Currier and Ives, Western Art Collection; **29 upper,** X-13904; **31 lower right,** X-652; **37 lower right,** Noah H. Rose, Z-49; **39, middle right,** Eagan, X-21568; **41 lower,** X-21974; **42,** Salsbury collection, Buffalo Bill's Wild West Show, NS-259; **43 upper left,** Salsbury collection, Buffalo Bill's Wild West Show, NS-242; **42–43,** Salsbury collection, Buffalo Bill's Wild West Show; photographs, A.R. Dresser; album no. 2, NS-455. All courtesy (detail) Denver Public Library, Western History Collection.

4, Brady-Handy Collection, LC-BH8301-1371; **9 upper right,** LC-B8184-2017; **37 lower middle,** "A wild western Amazon. The noted Belle Starr is arrested ...," wood engraving in *The National Police Gazette,* May 22, 1866, p. 16, LC-USZ62-63912. All courtesy Library of Congress/Famous People.

4–5 upper, *Trouble on the Horizon (Prospectors Discover an Indian Camp),* oil painting by Charles Russell, 1893; **7 upper right,** *Trouble on the Pony Express,* oil painting by Frank Tenney Johnson, ca.1910–1920; **10–11,** *The Forty-Niners,* oil painting by Oscar E. Berninghaus, n.d.; **17 lower right,** *Captured,* oil painting by Frederic Remington, 1899; **24–25 upper,** *Cowpunching Sometimes Spells Trouble,* oil painting by Charles Russell, 1889; **28–29 lower,** *Utica (A Quiet Day in Utica),* oil painting by Charles Russell, 1907; **38–39,** *The Hold Up (The Ambush),* oil painting by William Robinson Leigh, 1903. All courtesy Sid Richardson Collection of Western Art, Fort Worth, Texas.

5 lower right, Smithsonian Institution/Timothy H. O'Sullivan, NWDNS-106-WB-305; **5 lower middle,** John K. Hillers, Department of the Interior, Geological Survey, Office of the Chief Topographical Engineer, NWDNS-57-PE-110; **9 upper left,** Department of the Interior, National Park Service (II), NWDNS-79-M-1B-3; **13 left,** O'Sullivan, Select Audiovisual Records, Photographs of the American West: 1861–1912, #120, 77-KN-127; **16,** Select Audiovisual Records: Pictures of the Civil War, #163, 20OS-CA-10; **18,** David F. Barry, Department of Defense, Department of the Army, Office of the Chief Signal Officer, NWDNS-111-SC-85728; **21 right middle,** George N. Barnard and James F. Gibson, Select Audiovisual Records: Pictures of the Civil War, #15, 90-CM-385; **21 lower left,** Alfred A. Hart, Select Audiovisual Records: Photographs of the American West: 1861–1912, #16, 165-XS-28; **21 lower right,** Select Audiovisual Records: Photographs of the American West: 1861–1912, #17, 30-N-36-2994; **22–23,** War Department, NWDNS-165-XS-27; **26 lower,** Joseph F. Glidden, Department of the Interior. Patent Office, NWCTC-241-PATENT-157124; **27 lower left,** Kennett, Select Audiovisual Records: Photographs of the American West: 1861–1912, #179, 233-TRP-42; **27 lower right,** C.P. Rich, Select Audiovisual Records: Photographs of the American West: 1861–1912, #136, 48-RST-7B-77; **28,** Lubkin, Select Audiovisual Records: Photographs of the American West: 1861–1912, #187, 115-JQ-390; **31 upper,** C.S. Fly, Select Audiovisual Records: Photographs of the American West: 1861–1912, #185, 111-SC-93344; **32,** Jackson, Select Audiovisual Records: Photographs of the American West: 1861–1912, #153, 57-HS-716; **33 lower left,** Select Audiovisual Records: Photographs of the American West: 1861–1912, #181, 48-RST-7B-97; **33 lower right,** S.J. Morrow, Select Audiovisual Records: Photographs of the American West: 1861–1912, #155, 165-FF-2F-15; **35 upper left,** Camillus S. Fly, Select Audiovisual Records: Photographs of the American West: 1861–1912, #82, 111-SC-94129; **35 upper right,** C. Hart Merriam, Select Audiovisual Records: Photographs of the American West: 1861–1912, #83, 22-WB-886; **40,** Mathew Brady Photograph of Civil War-Era Personalities and Scenes, War Department, Office of the Chief Signal Officer, NWDNS-111-B-3202; **40–41 upper,** Select Audiovisual Records: Photographs of the American West: 1861–1912, #84, 111-SC-93343. All courtesy U.S. National Records and Archives Administration (NARA).

6–7 lower, John C.H. Grabill, LC-DIG-ppmsc-02598 DLC; **8,** *The scout Buffalo Bill, Hon. W.F. Cody* by Paul Frenzeny, lithograph by Forbes Co., LC-USZC4-6424; **13 right,** John C.H. Grabill, LC-DIG-ppmsc-02598; **15 lower right,** *Judge David S. Terry, stabbing S.A. Hopkins, of the vigilance committee, San Francisco, Cal., 1856,* LC-USZ62-70565; **25 lower left,** John C.H. Grabill, LC-DIG-ppmsc-02628; **33 upper,** Lawrence & Houseworth, LC-USZ62-17739. All courtesy Library of Congress/Prints and Photographs Division.

15 upper right, letter, California vigilante committee to John Stephens, September 5, 1856. Courtesy Library of Congress/Manuscript Division/American Memory/Isaac D. Bluxome Collection http://memory.loc.gov/mss/mcc/066/0001.jpg.

19 upper left, Charles Marion Russell, *War Council on the Plains* (62.85), Collection of Glenbow Museum, Calgary, Canada.

25 lower right, Courtesy, Colorado Historical Society, detail, CHS.J4283, William Henry Jackson.

37 lower left, W.B. Lawson, *Jesse James at Long Branch,* 1898, mtfrb dn003. Courtesy Library of Congress/Rare Book and Special Collections Division/Meeting of Frontiers.